Intents and Purposes

Story and Illustrations
By
Tonia Colleen Martin

Graphic Design
by
Jennifer Rose Triebwasser

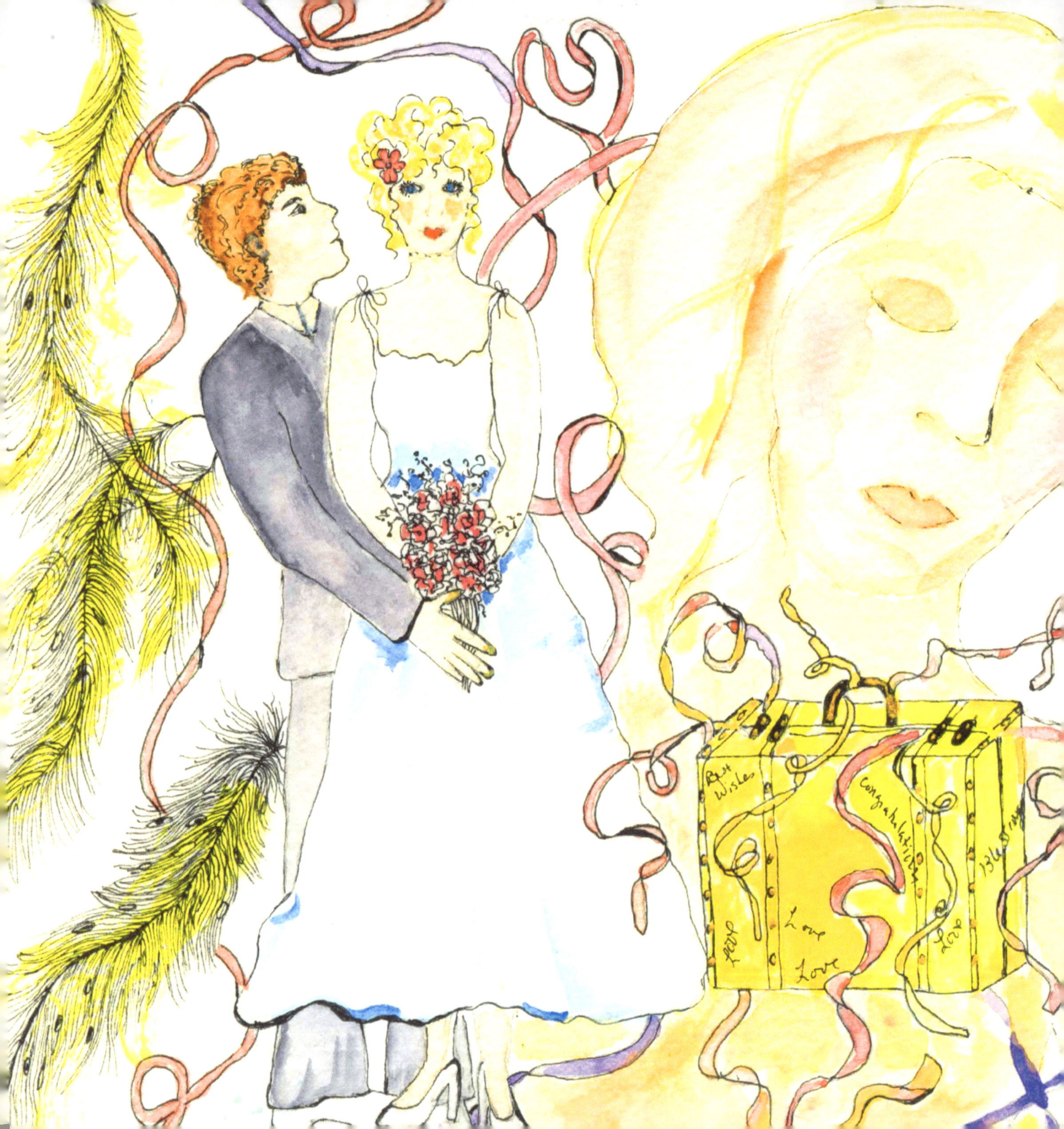
Best Wishes
Congratulations
Blessings
Peace
Love
Love
Love

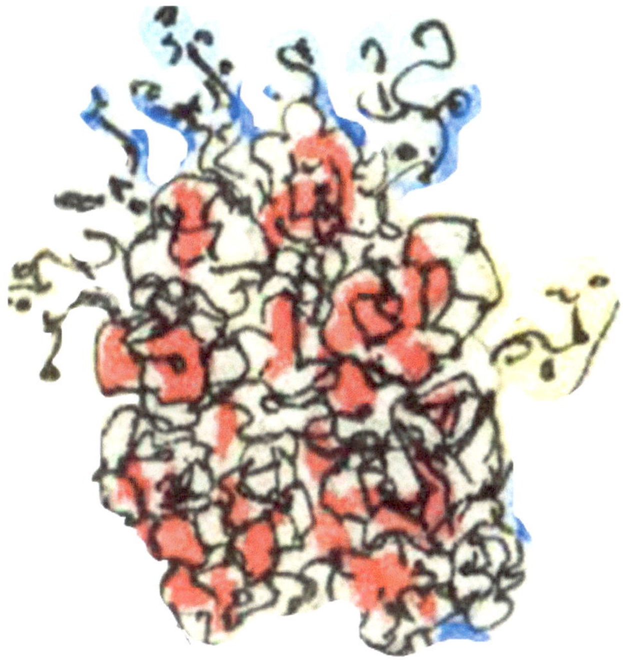

She carries a glass bouquet. Imagine.
Breakable blooms.
Blooms carried like sky
hooks to love.

It is a happy occasion.
But there are tears.
Wept and unwept.
The tears are here.

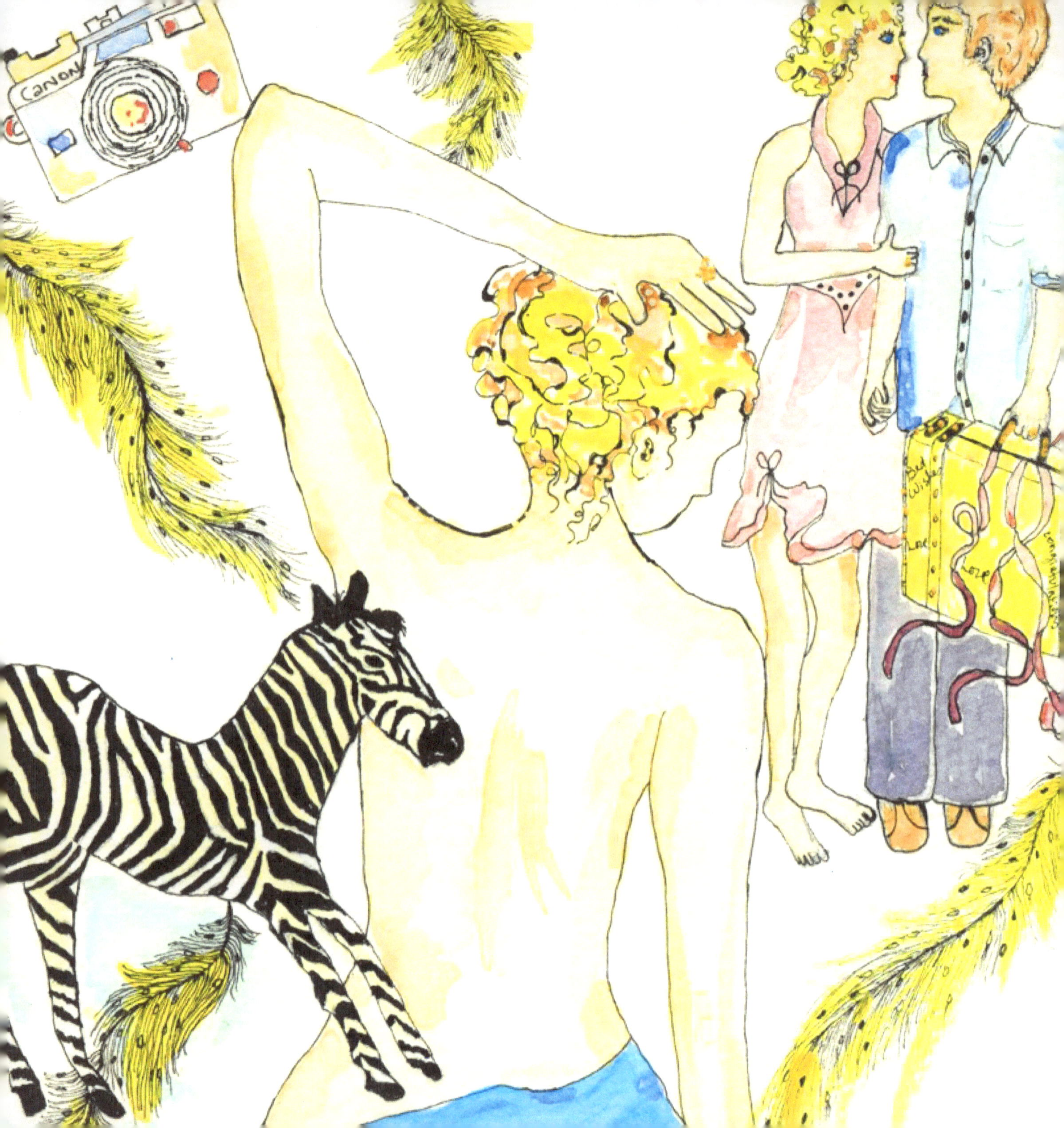

CANON

She knows nothing. Less
than nothing.
This is what she knows.
She has agreed to what
she does not know, to what
she believes will be easy.

Something black.
Something white.

Knowing she knows nothing
happens later. This is now.
Now she does not cry.
She leaves her weeping behind.
Behind is where
her weeping remains.

A ring is slipped on her finger.
A circle of gold.
And then his hand is also
captured with gold.
Pictures are taken.
Pictures remember.
Nothing is needed
to help them forget.
Forgetting is easier
than remembering.

Between them swings a suitcase.

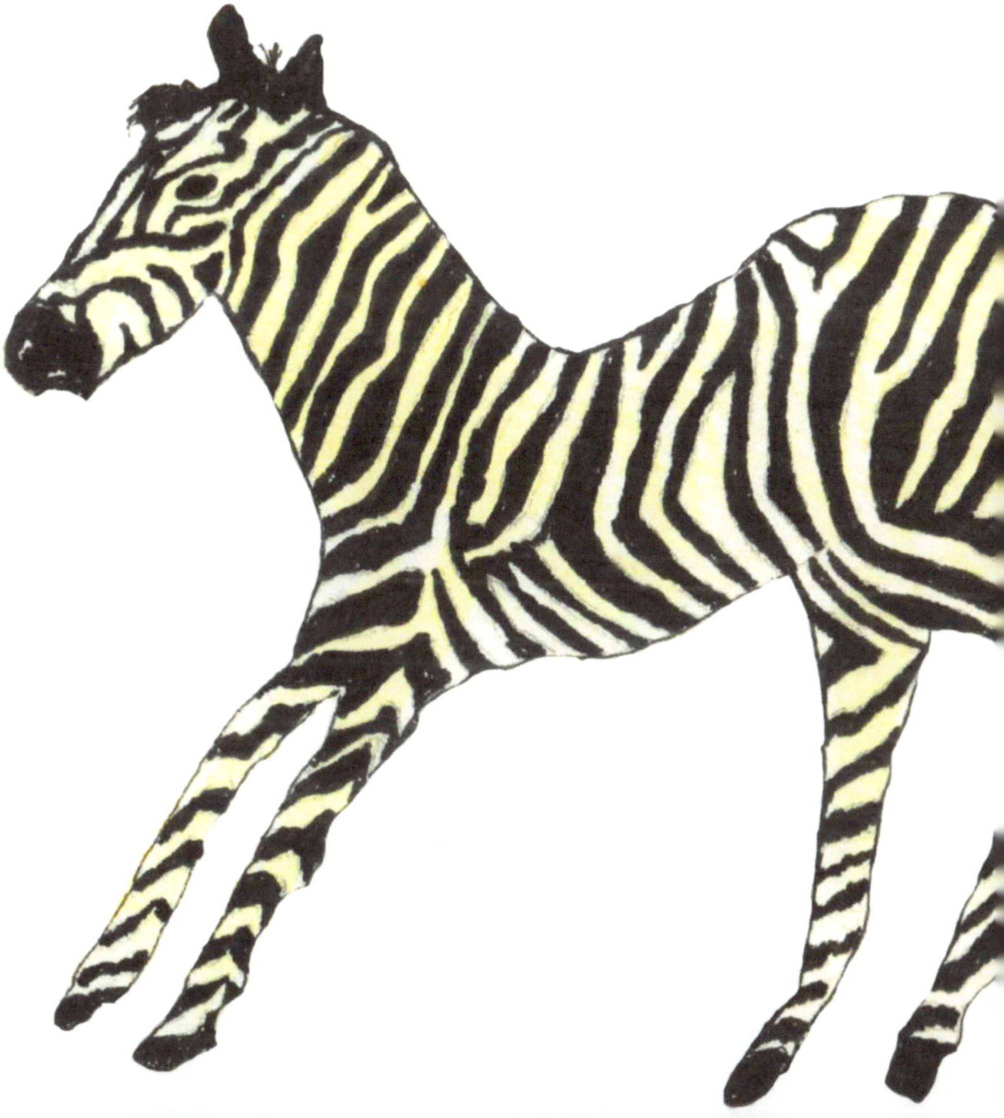

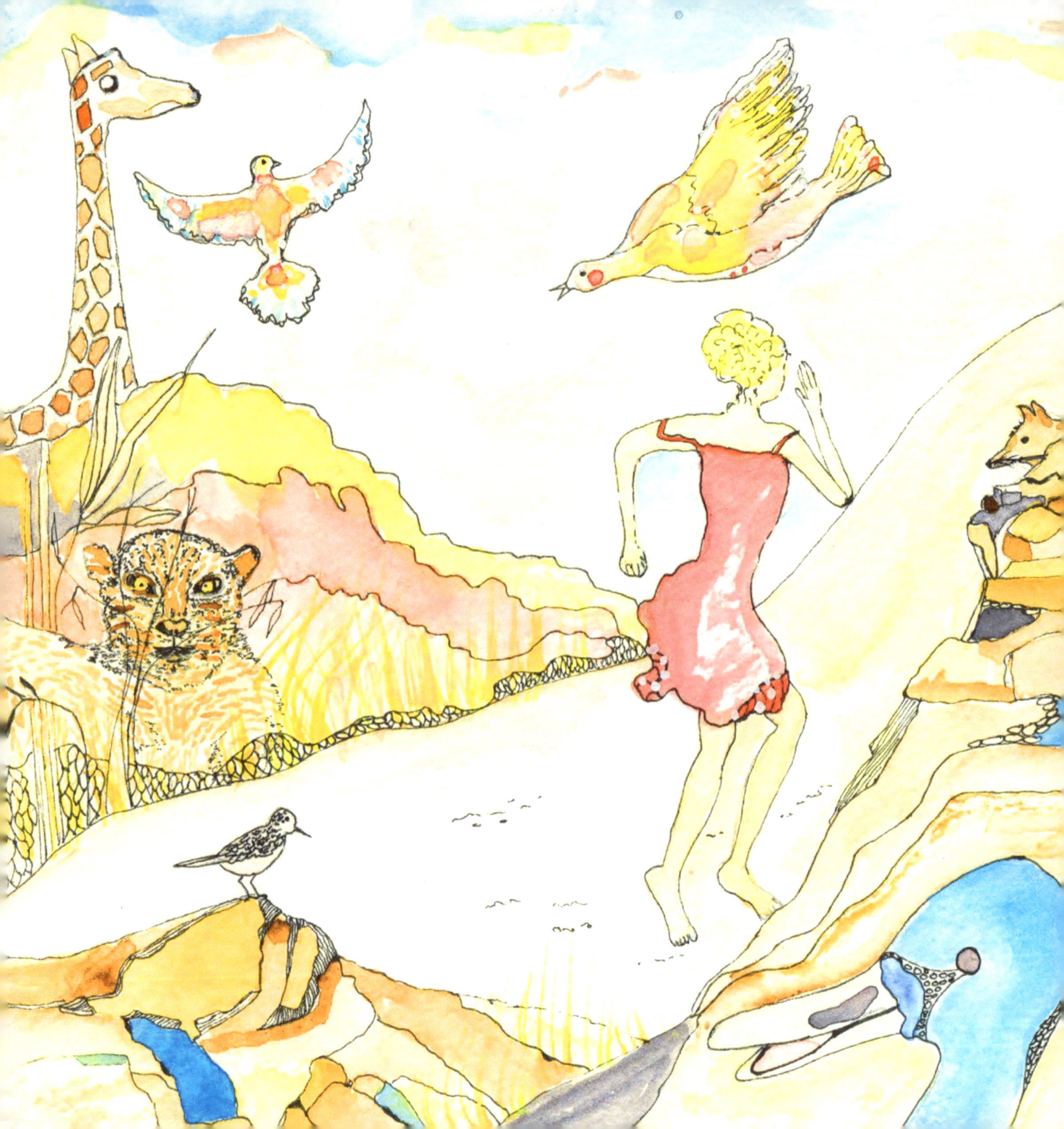

The suitcase is as close to yellow as any other color.
For a surprise, the sisters wrap it with ribbons.
The brothers carve blessings into its side.

The lovers latch arms. This is why they think
they are strong, why they believe they have power.
Strength resides in their arms.
They embrace everything. Lift much.
Carry more.

The way is surprisingly rough.
She doesn't mention the presence of hills, ignores
the ruts, sees only small declivities. No ditches, no
peaks, certainly no cliffs.

The road narrows, erupts with trees.
An unexpected wind sweeps down.
Years of running begin.

To slow her down, wild animals appear.
Wild animals distract her.
She dare not stay, dare not linger.
Wild animals refuse to be tamed.

And then birds. Far off, now closer.
Finally, alarmingly near, in her face, her
hair, frisking her shoulders. An infantry
of feathers. Battalion of beaks.

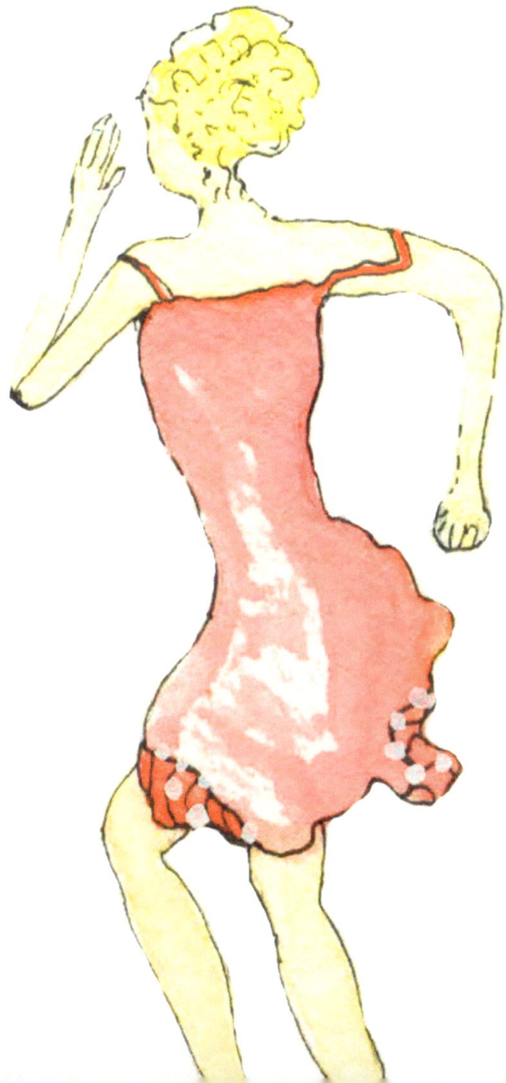

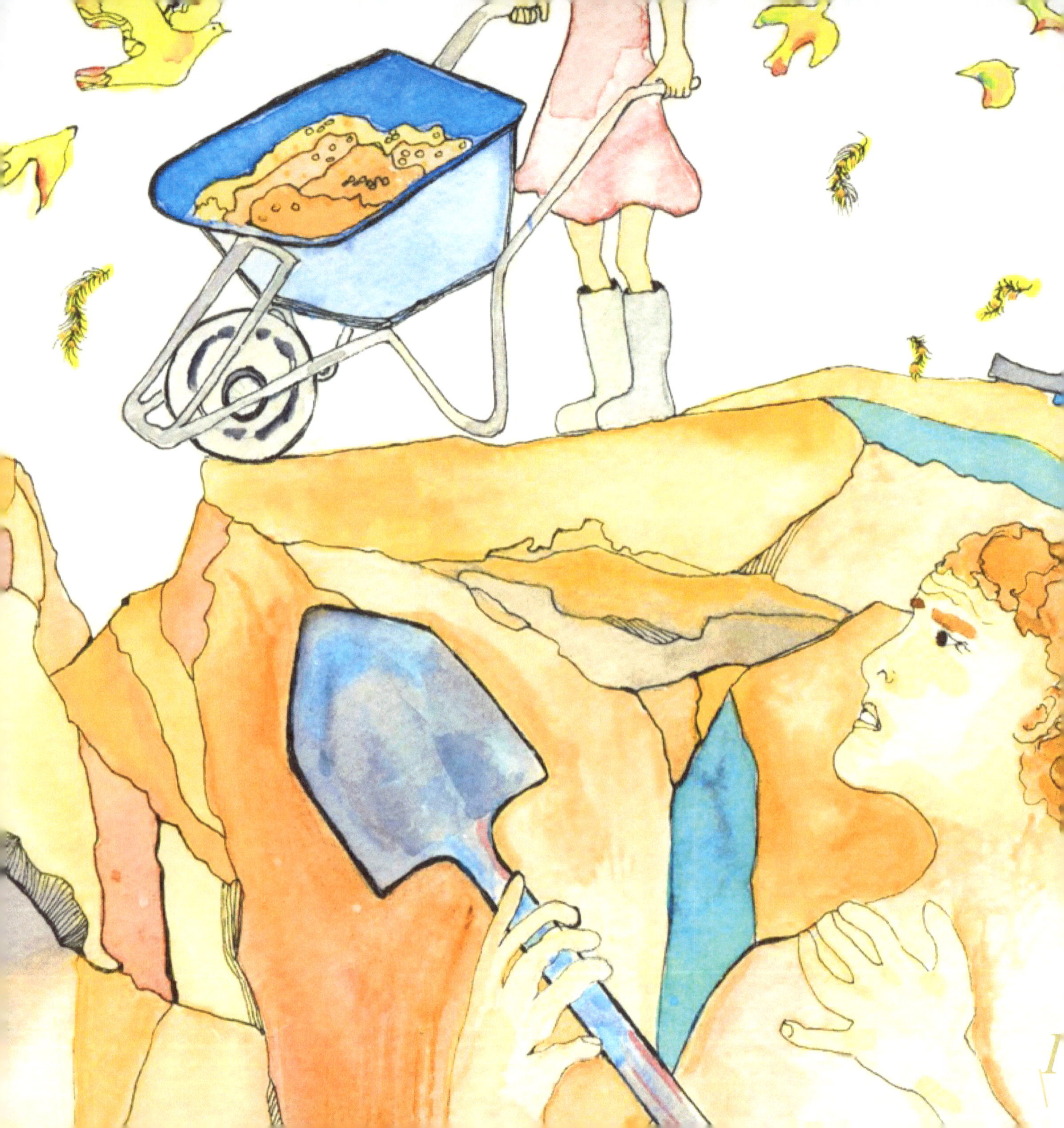

She is not at peace with flapping,
not at peace with pecking.

"Go. Take your feathers. Take your beaks."

But the birds remain. Before, she considered birds to be creatures of music, creatures of song. These birds do not sing. Music is not in them. Birds are the cause of their first fight. Not so much him, not so much her, but birds outside their influence. Birds they cannot cage or shoo away.

And so they cage themselves, shoo others away and dig elaborate tunnels. They borrow almost everything - shovels, picks, back hoes as well as dirt.

He digs. She carts away, gets rid of the evidence. Worry sets in. She considers how quickly a tunnel might crumble to a grave.

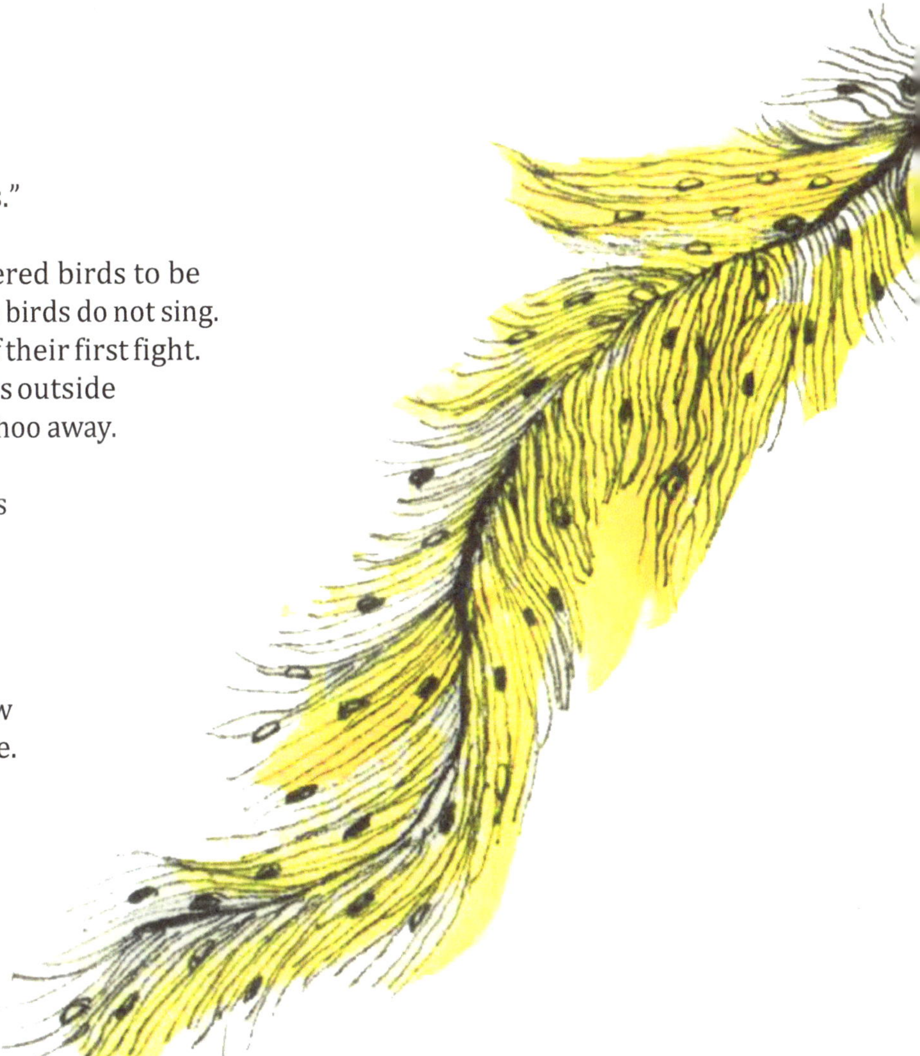

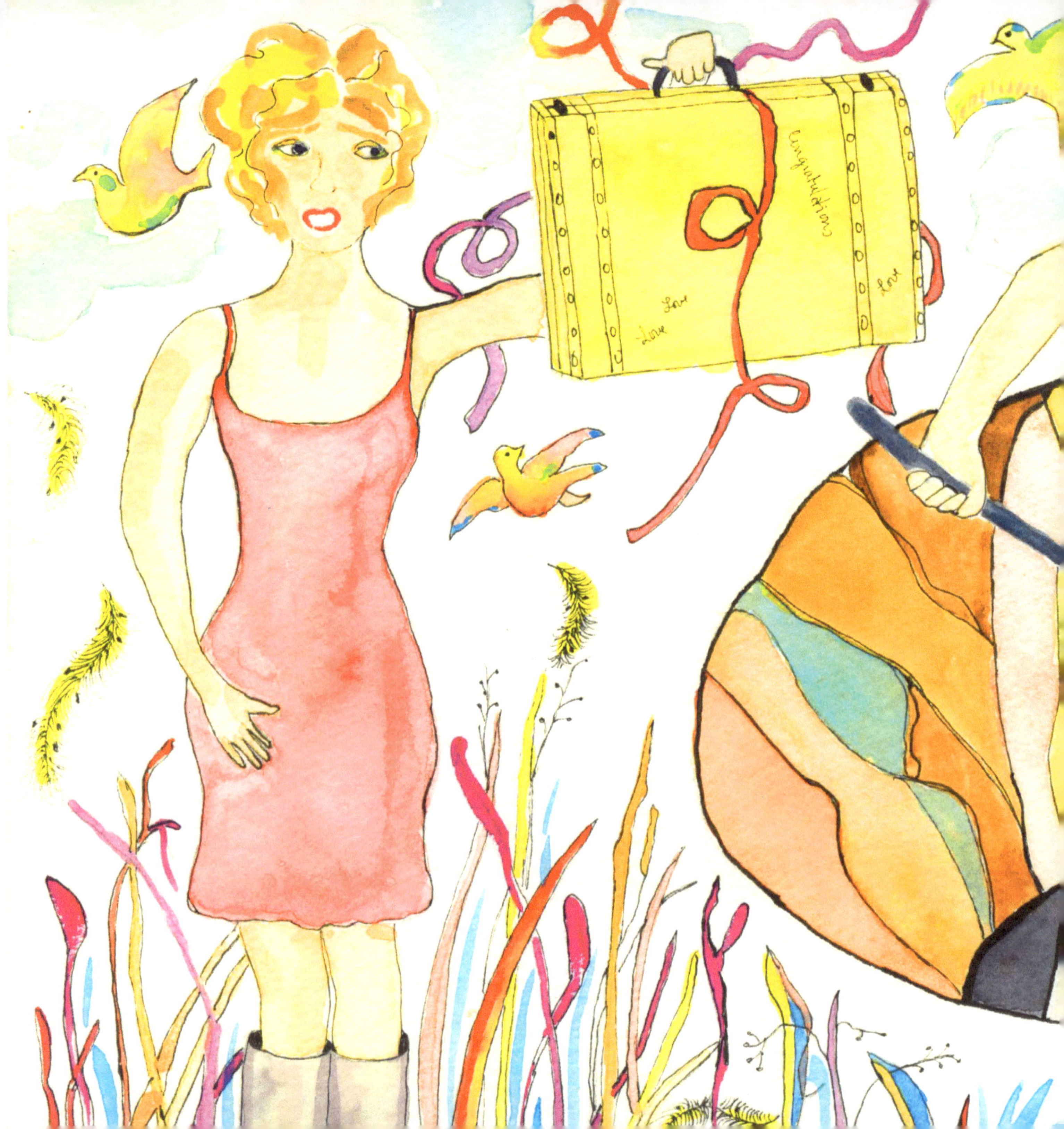
Congratulations
Love
Love
Love

"Remember," she says, waving the suitcase.

He eyes the suitcase, drops the pick, returns the shovel, remembers the sky, remembers desire.

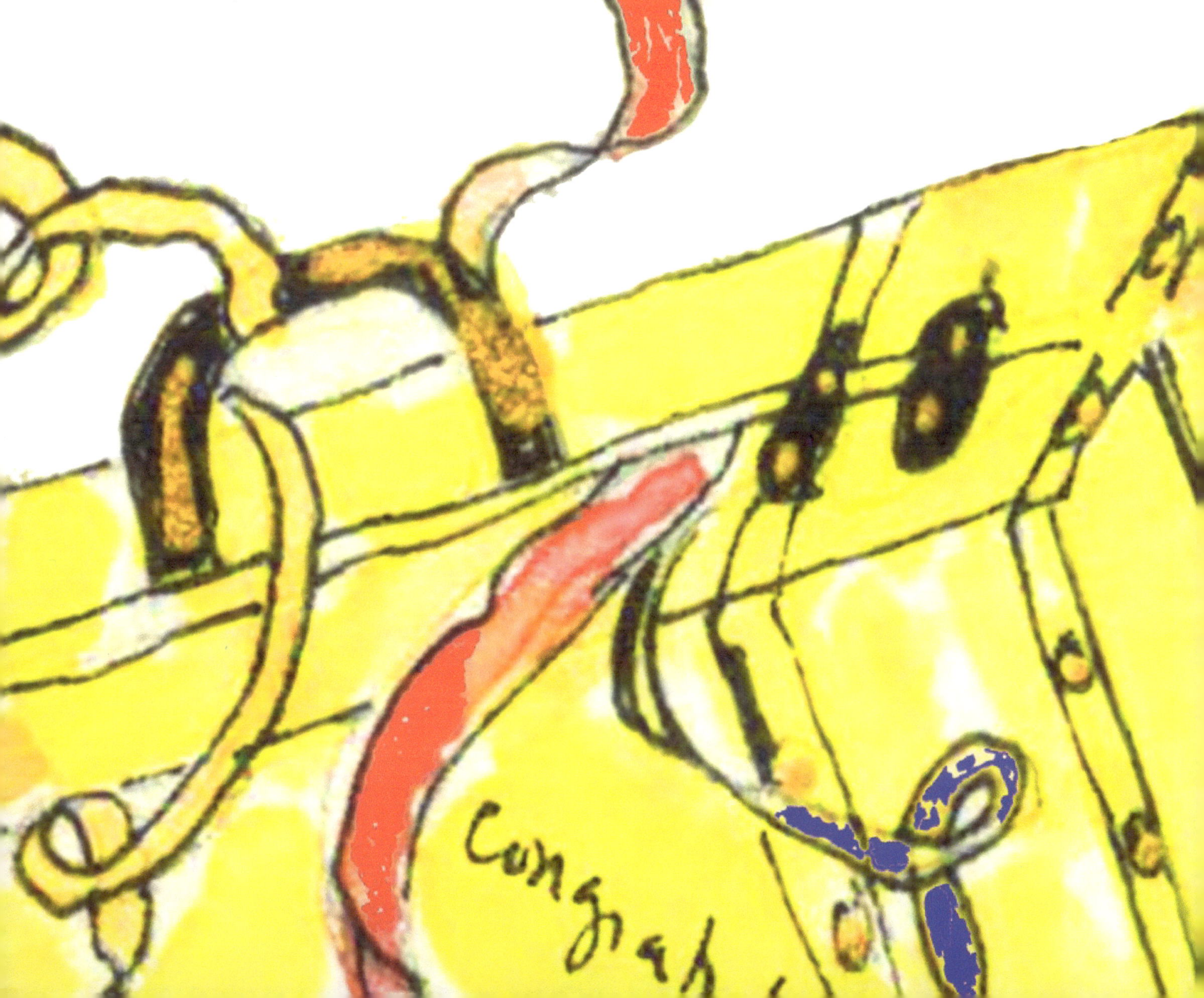

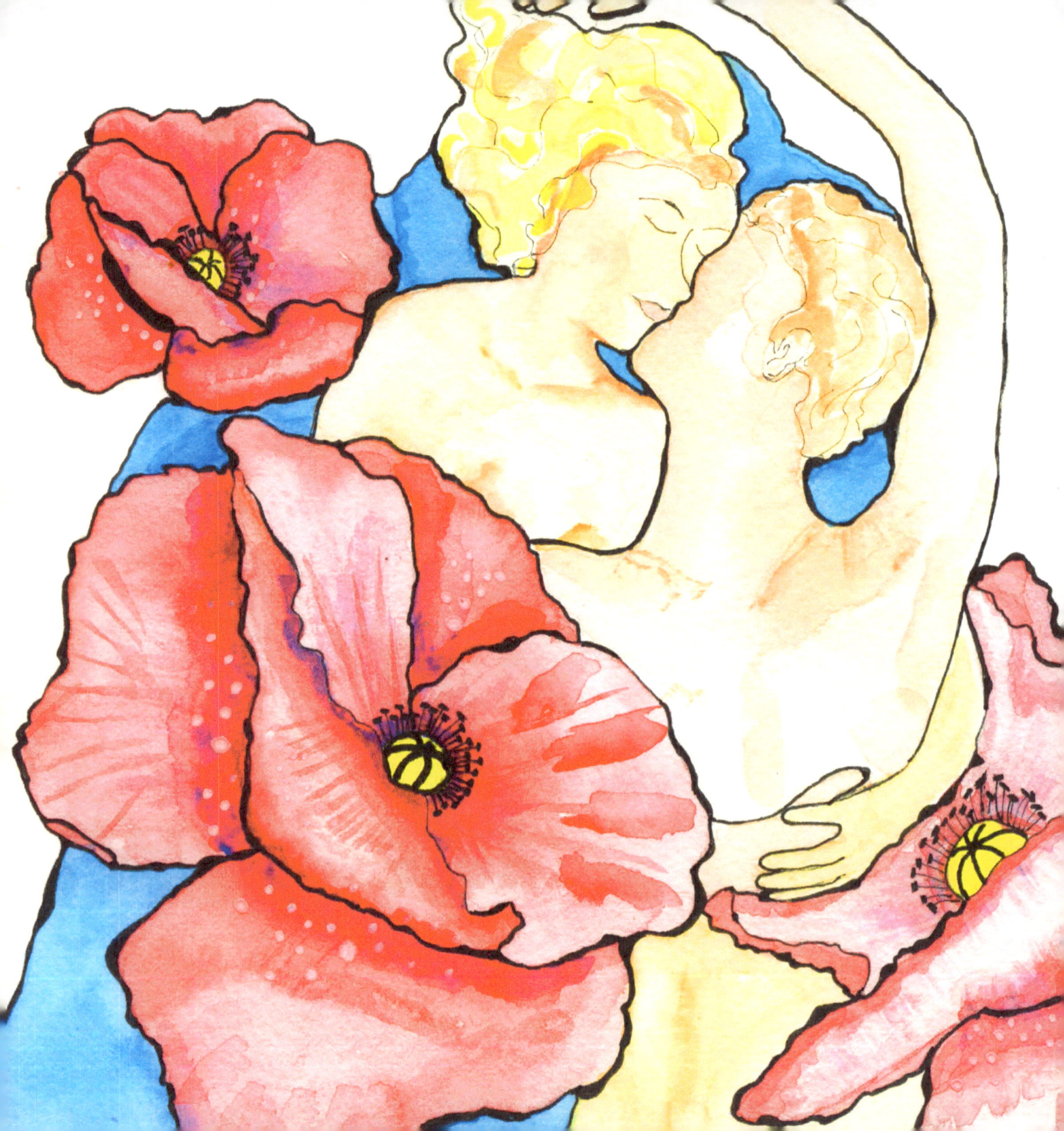

Together they are a flower. Open petals, visible stamens, scent of oceans fragrantly crashing.

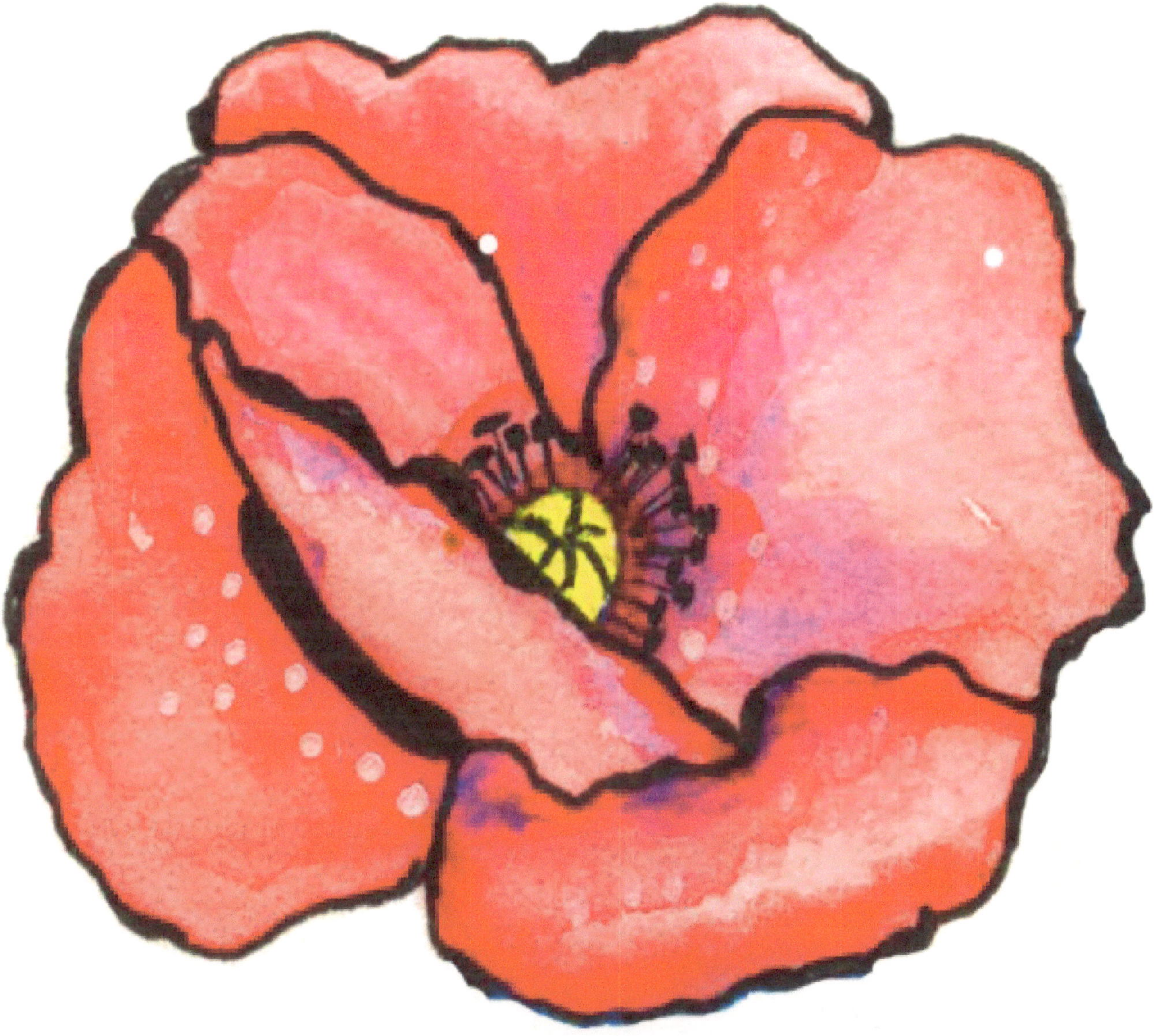

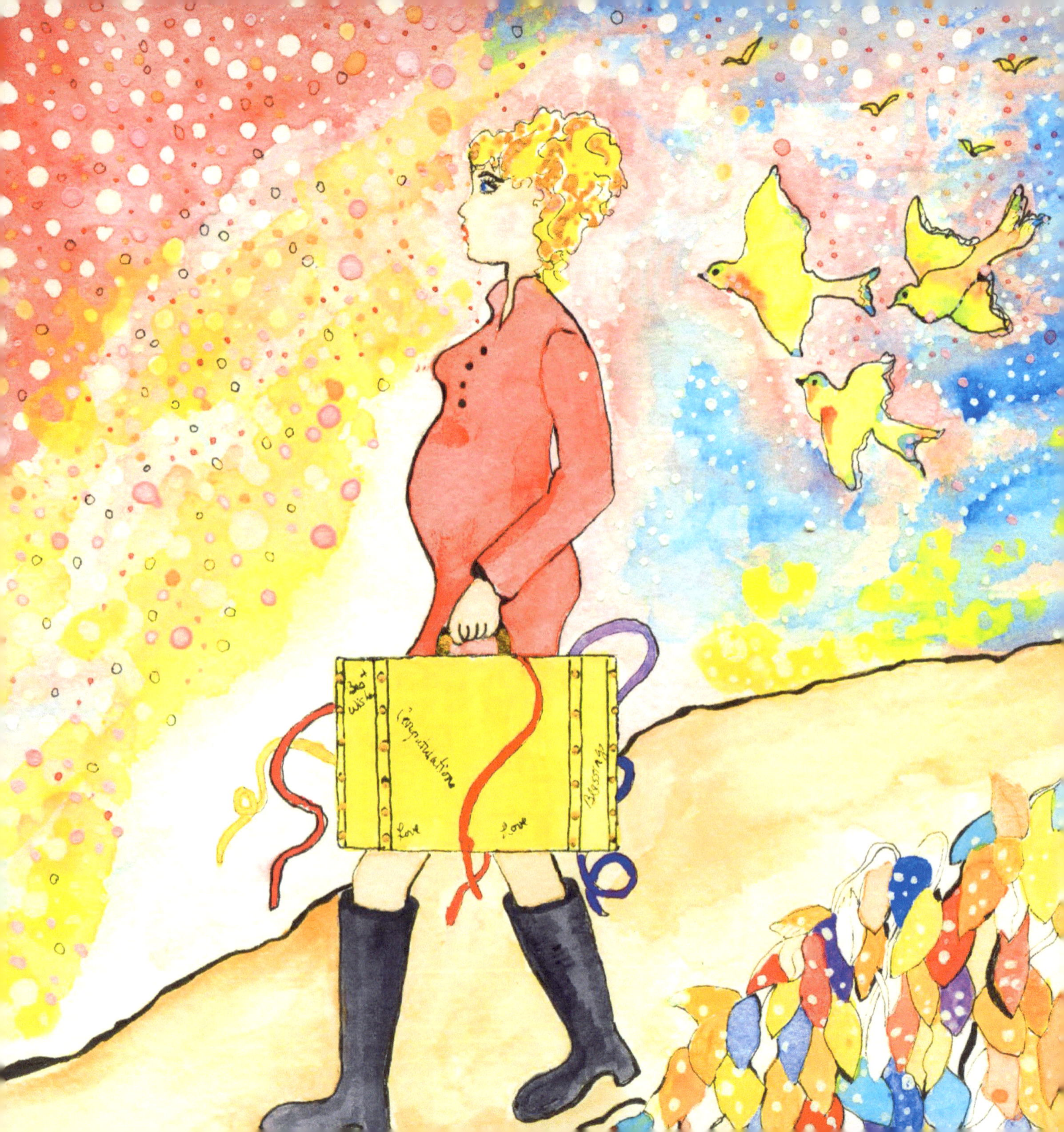

Best Wishes
Congratulation
Blessings
Love
Love

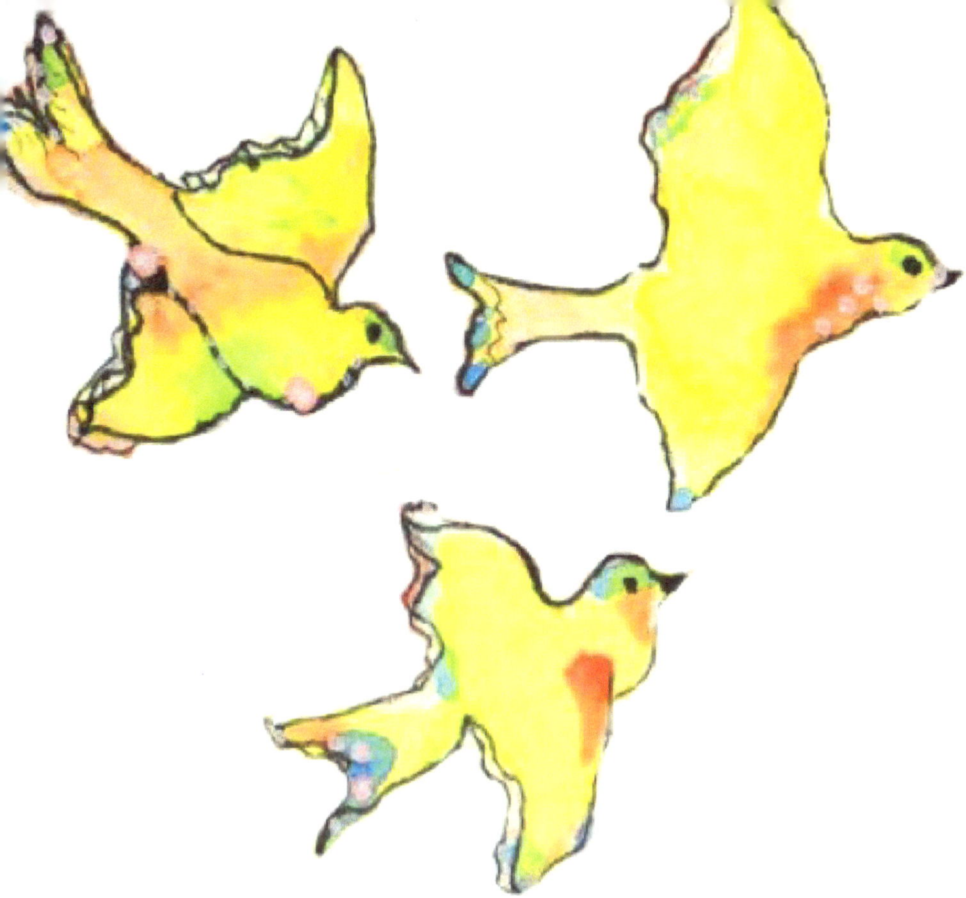

Spring arrives. She feels a lilting nudge, a small foot pushing, a small hand grasping. This second heart captures her.

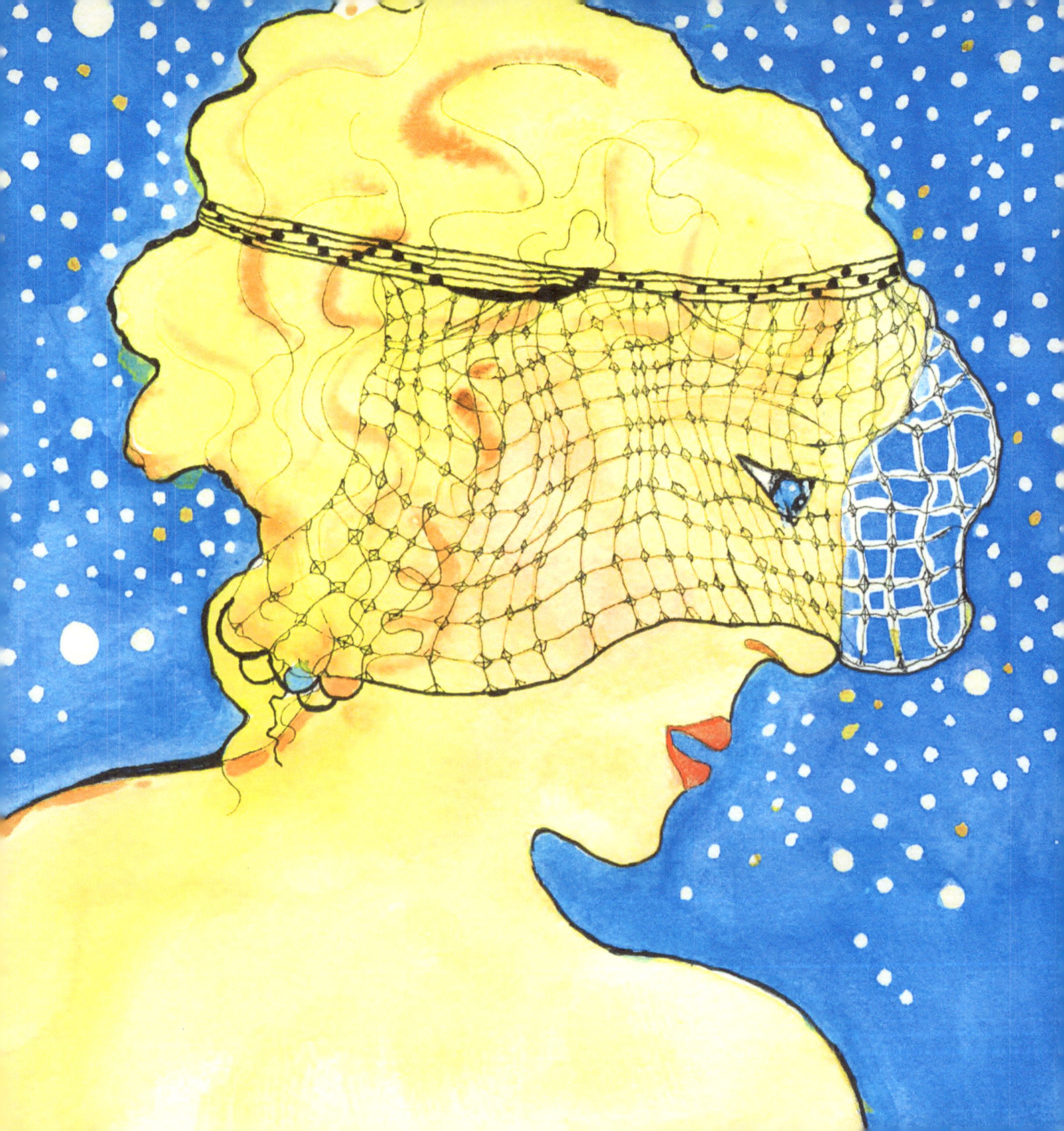

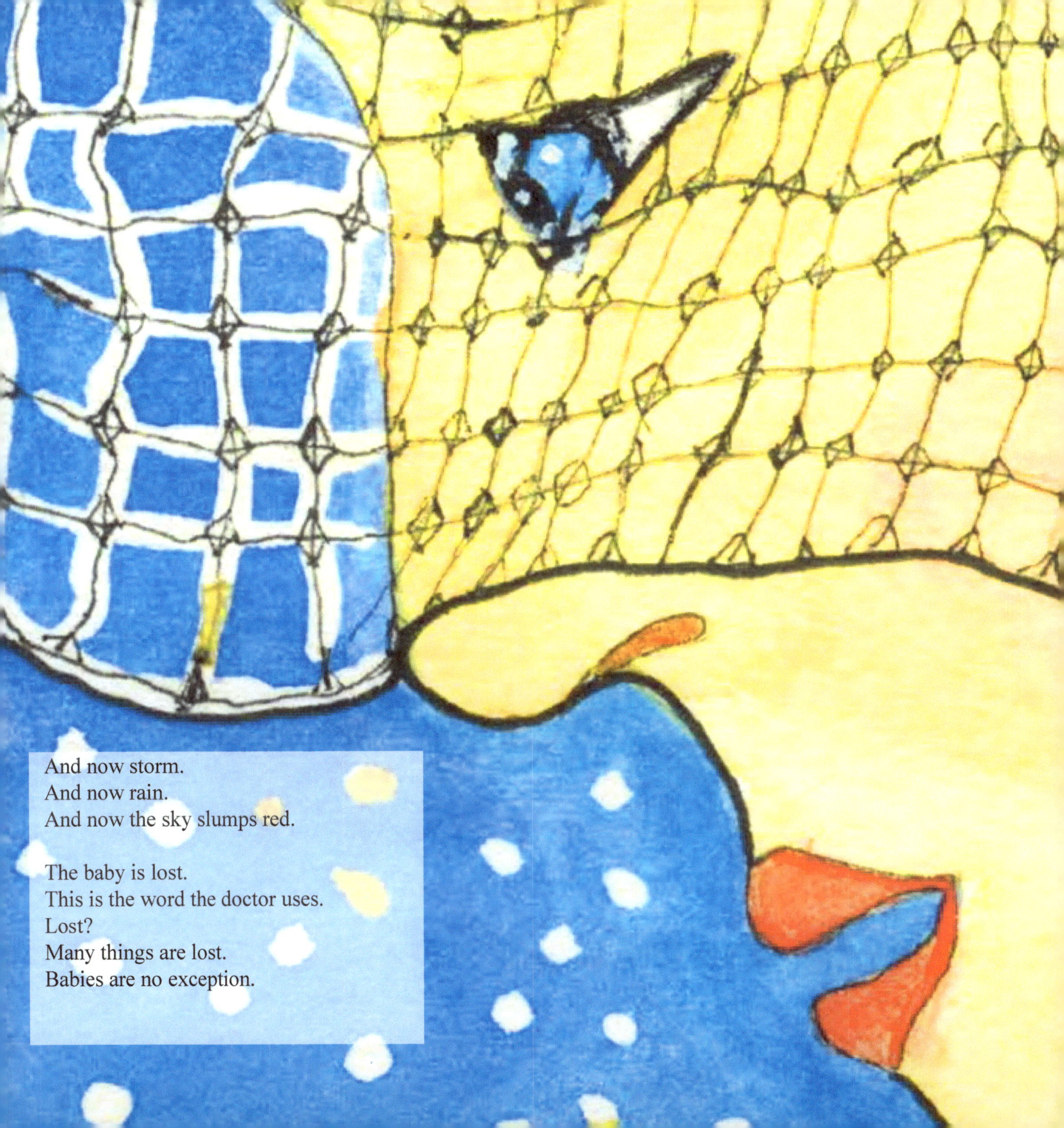

And now storm.
And now rain.
And now the sky slumps red.

The baby is lost.
This is the word the doctor uses.
Lost?
Many things are lost.
Babies are no exception.

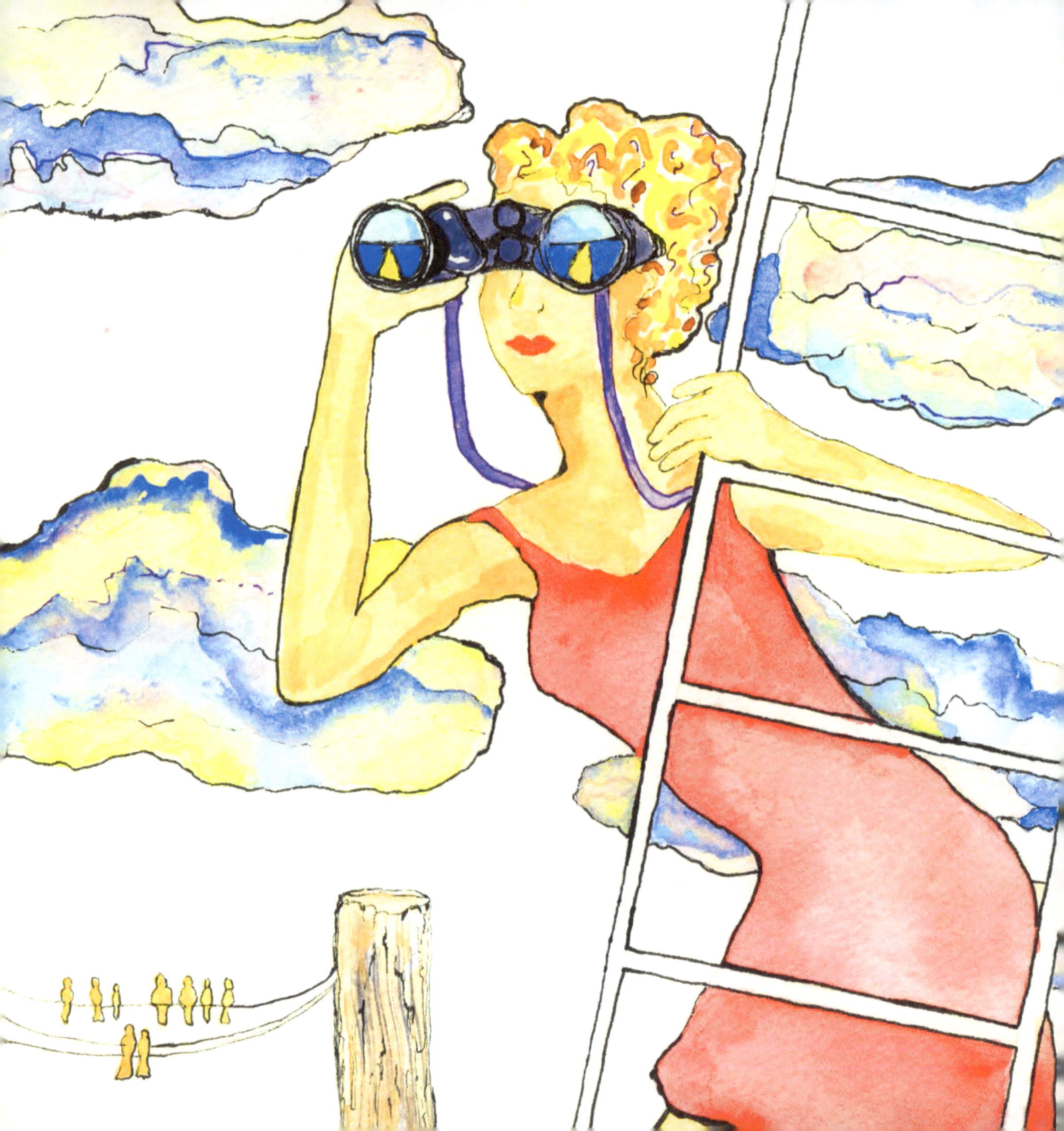

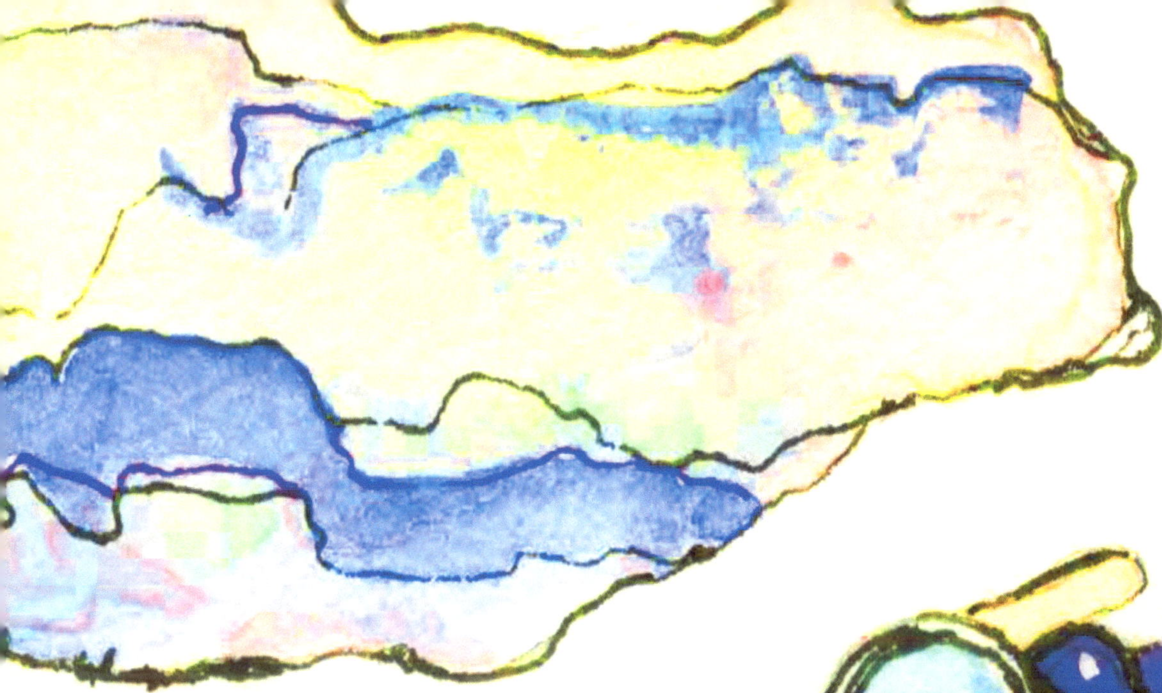

In this lostness, he goes missing too.
Where is he? He is other than here.
Finally he returns.
Shows up.
Is ready to move.
She feels his muscled arms.
She believes in his strength,
believes in his protection.

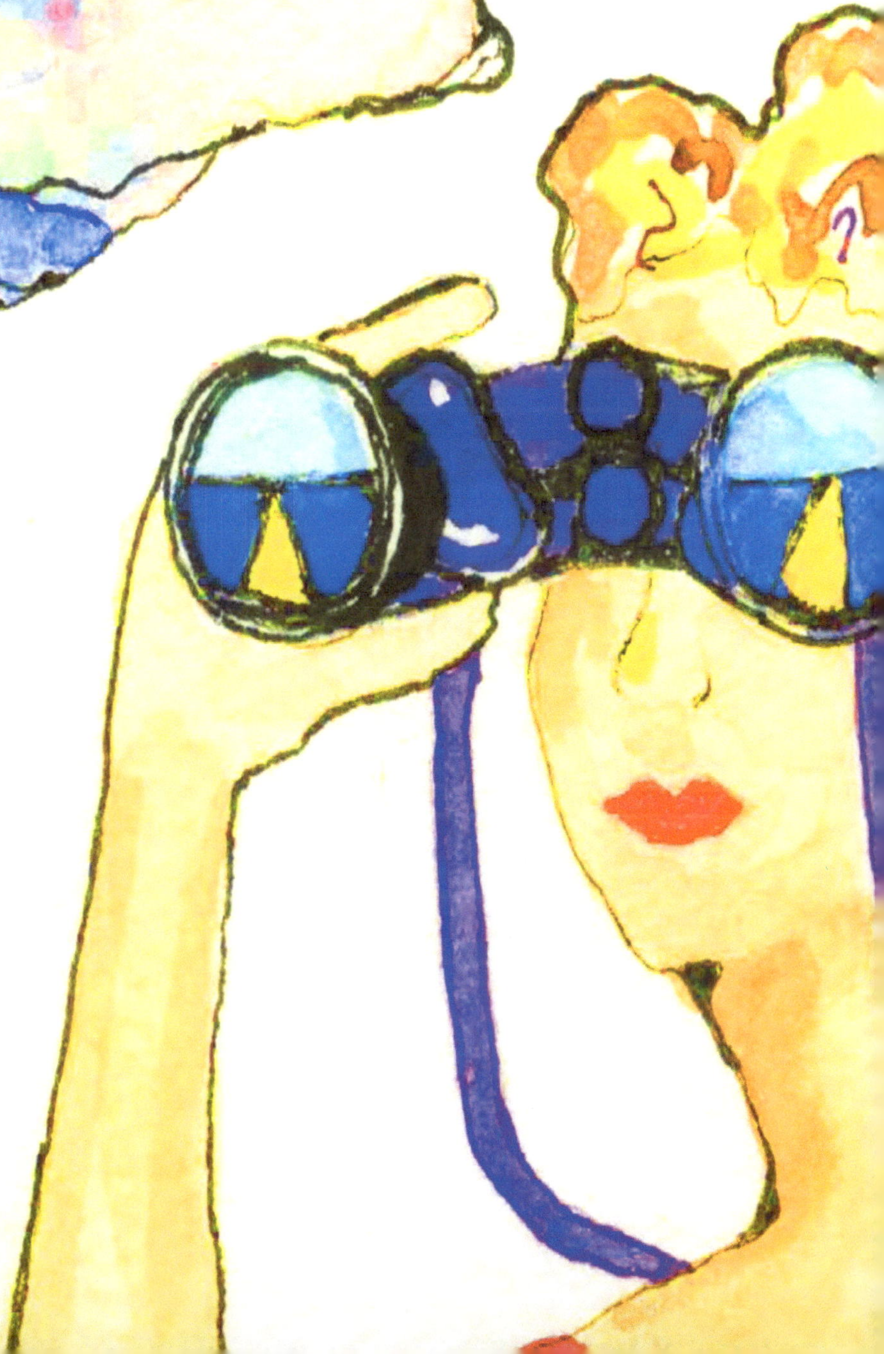

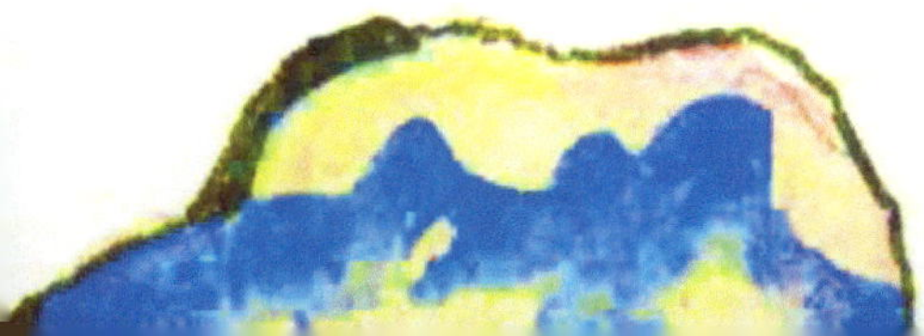

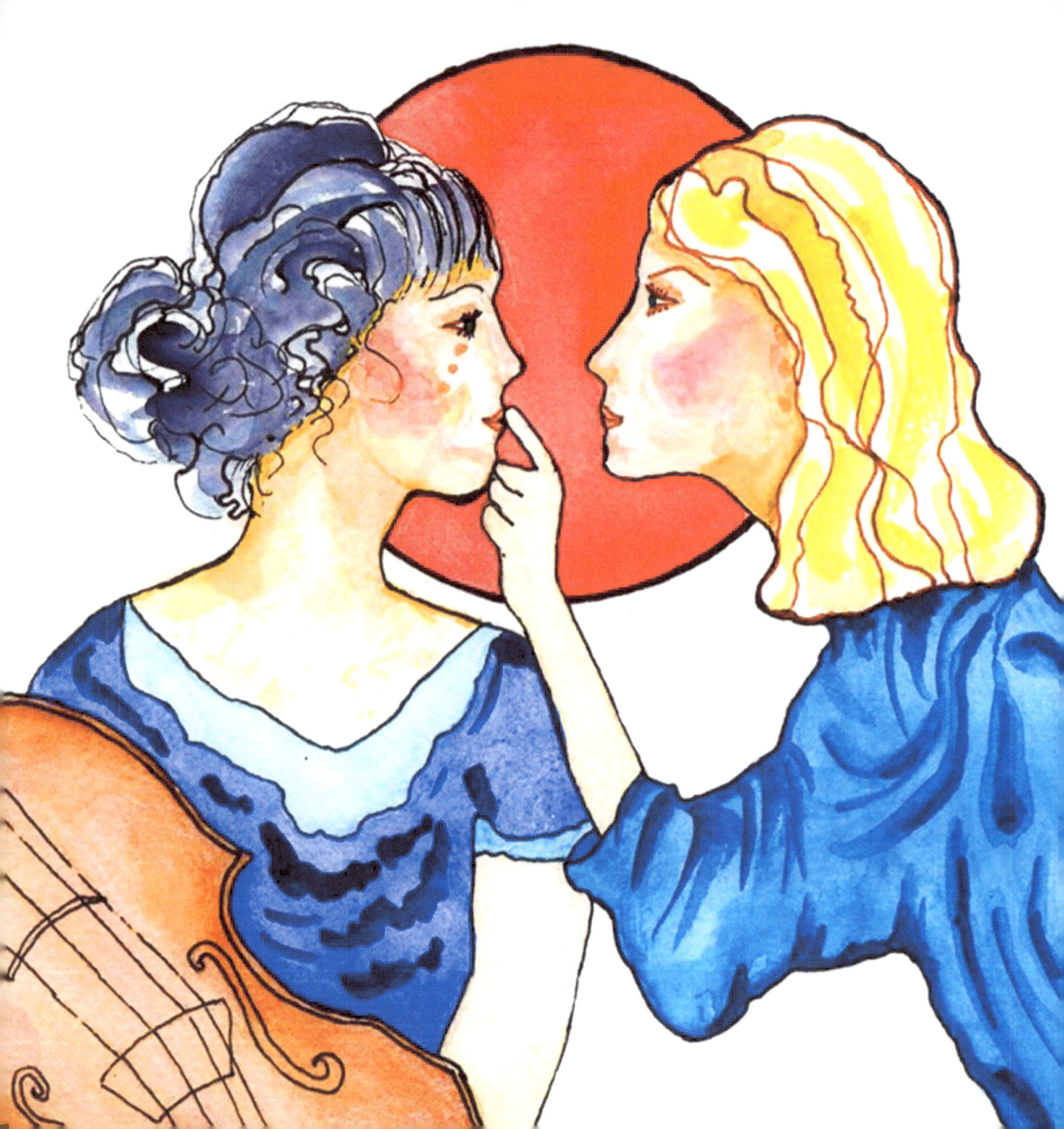

Time passes. More children.
First one. Then another.
The first daughter knows what not to say.
And the second daughter, she learns also.

Turning the house to smiles, the children protect
the lost language of their parents.

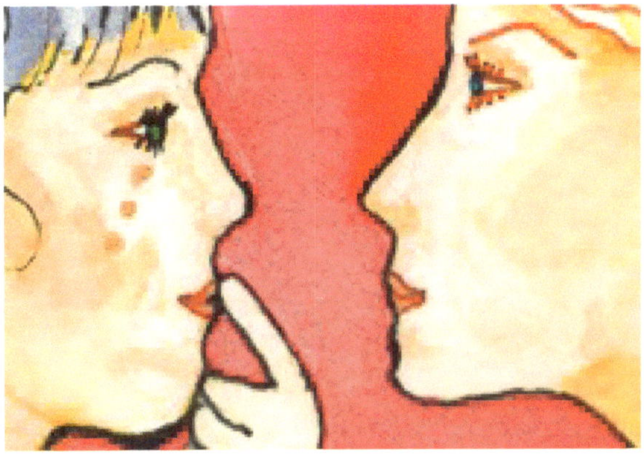

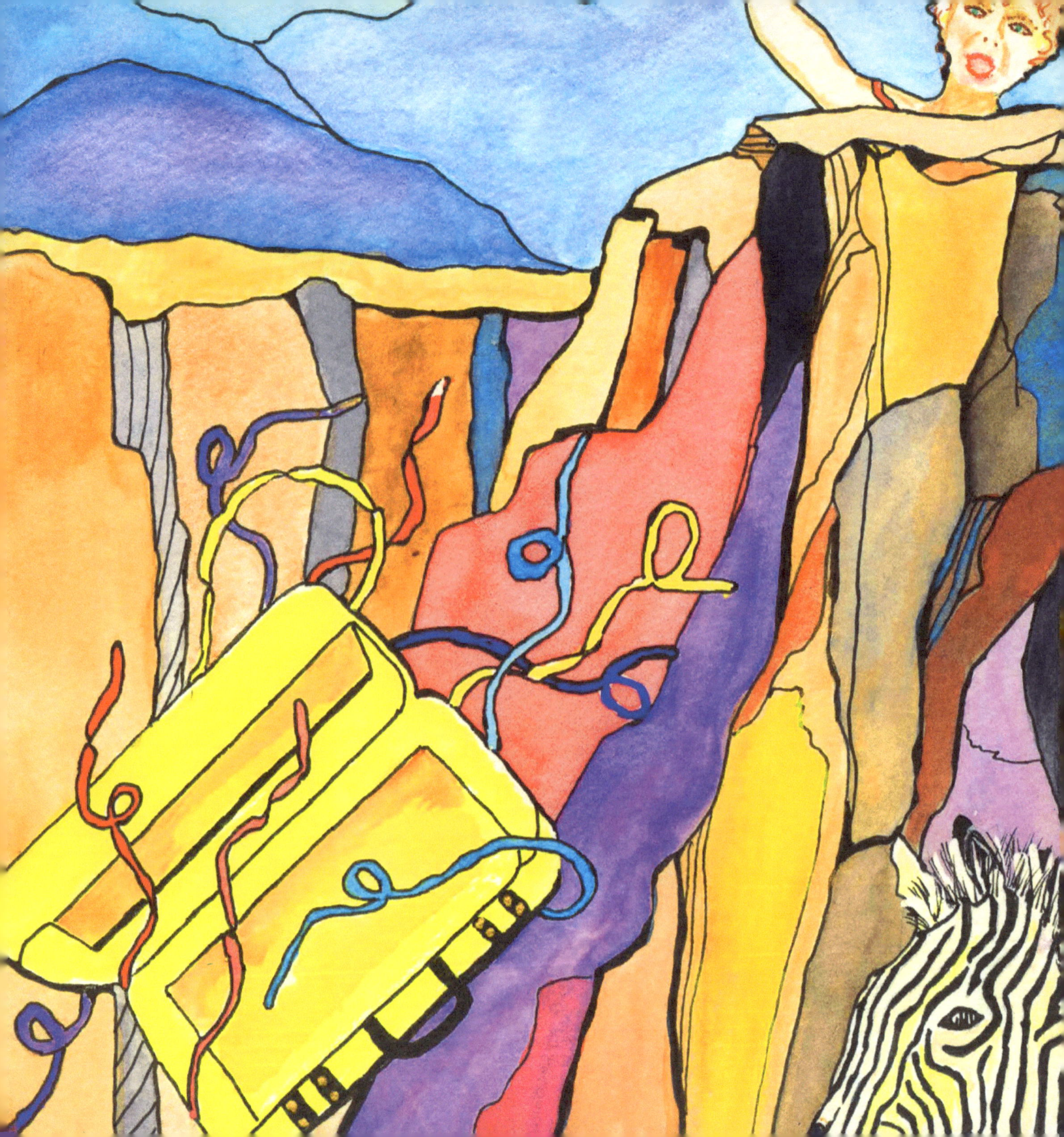

One day, she finds herself on a very steep
mountain. There should be warnings, a
large sign with an enormous black X.
Weary, panting, she mops her brow.
It is the dead of winter, sweat drenches her
and the suitcase is hers alone.

Against her dreams, against the black, against the white,
she calls forth the last dregs of strength, lets fly
the suitcase and wails. As the wailing leaves
her, it gathers such velocity, she realizes it has
always been in route.

Life scatters backwards, scatters forwards.
Nothing remains fixed. Photos,
furniture, jewelry, books, trust, and
credibility. Dead things as well as
living.

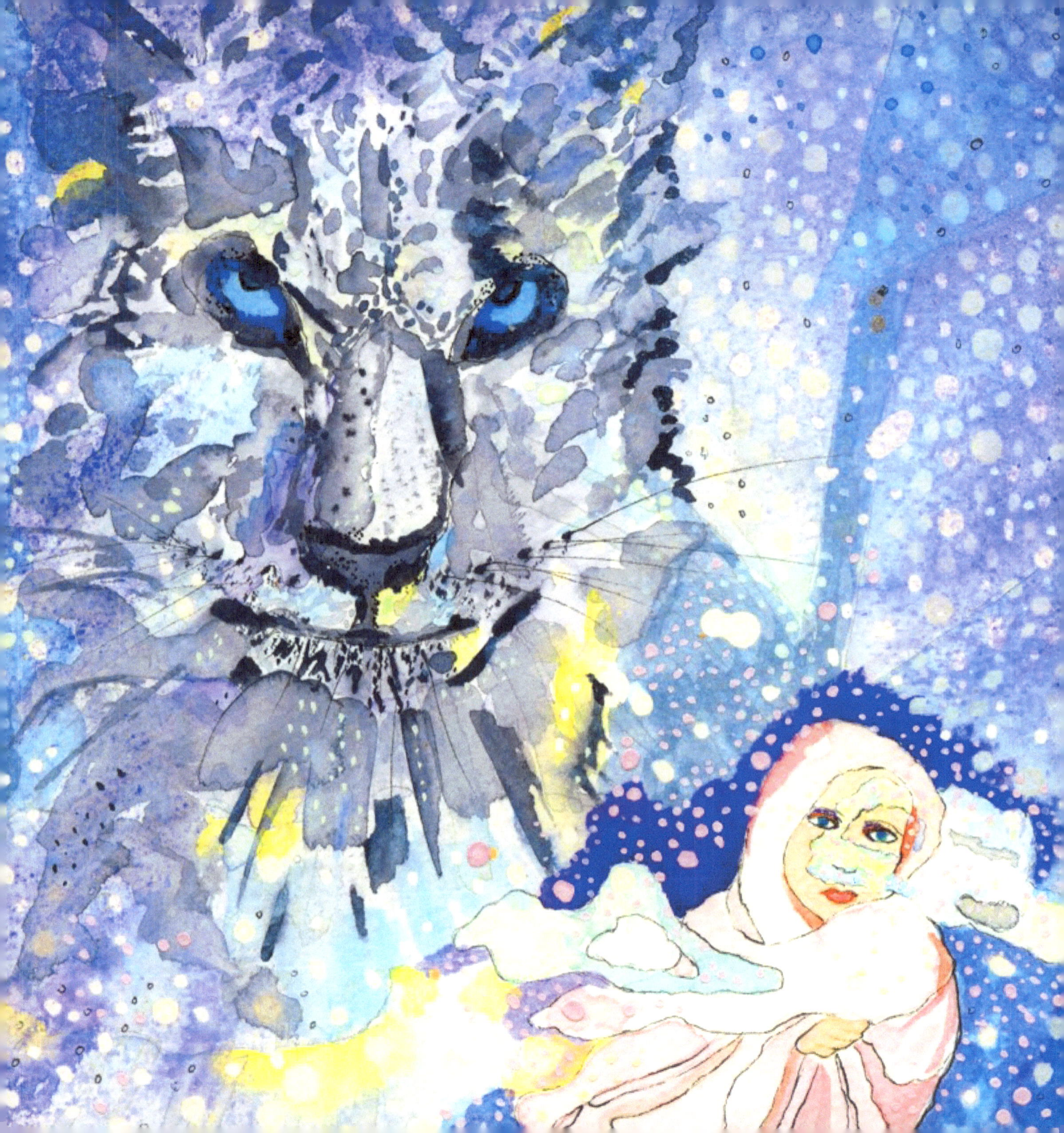

Leprous snow falls, devouring sun, devouring sky.
For lack of strength, she lies down, closes her eyes,
forgets how to be.

A voice calls out.
She opens her eyes and sees a fire. What
kind of fire burns in the snow? Lifting a
foot, she flings it forward,
lifts the other and flings it desperately ahead.

Finally, she feels warmth.
Always before she was cold. Cold, beyond shivers,
cold in the way of ice blankets,
in the way of numbness,
in the way of dead.

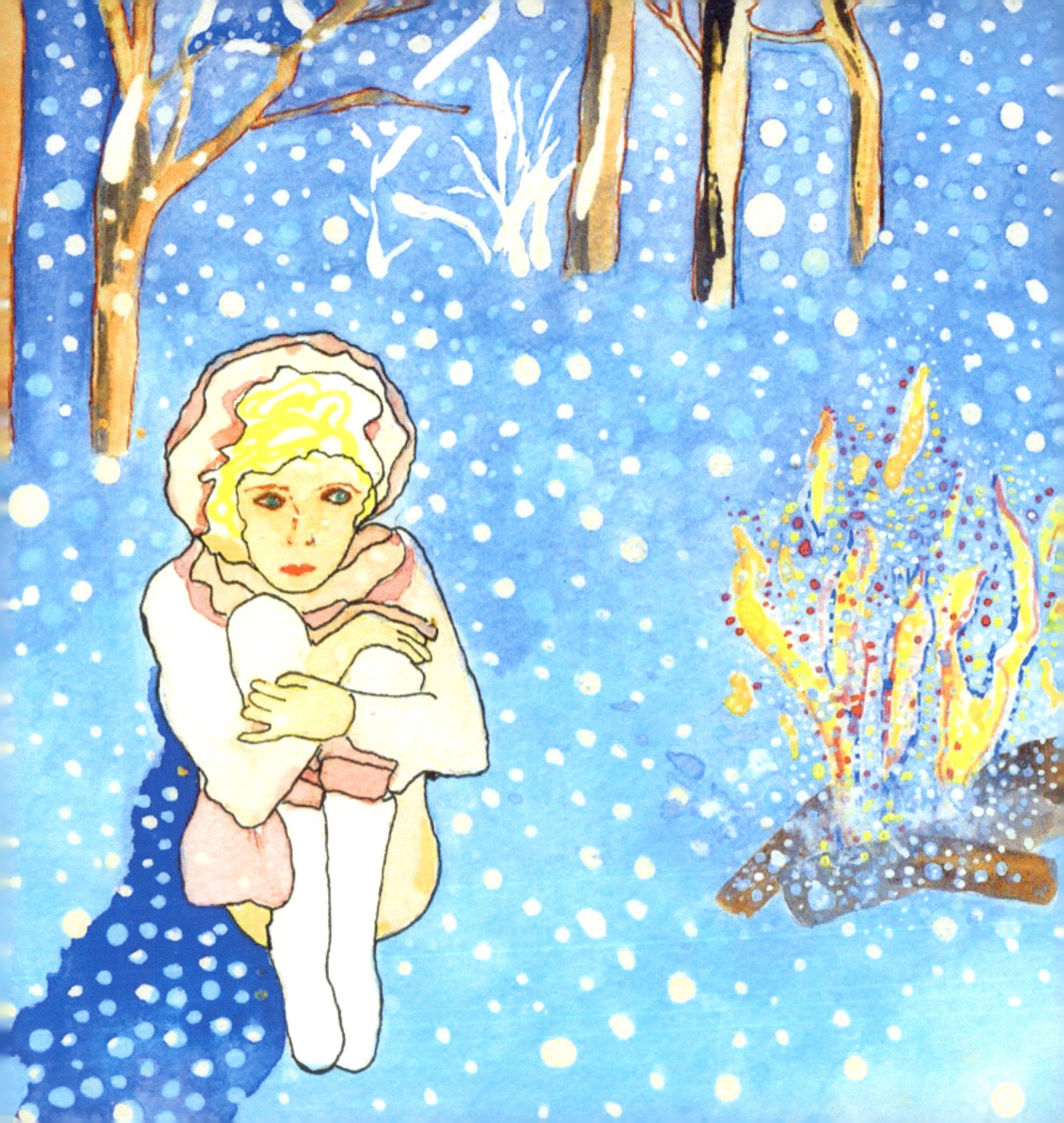

The fire bewilders her, enchants her. Mesmerized by the flames, she considers the fuel on which the fire feeds. Is the fire feeding on a suitcase? *The* suitcase?

This is the form her bewilderment takes - the form of a question. With the same words she can make a statement. But she asks a question.

The answer is yes, the suitcase is feeding the fire.

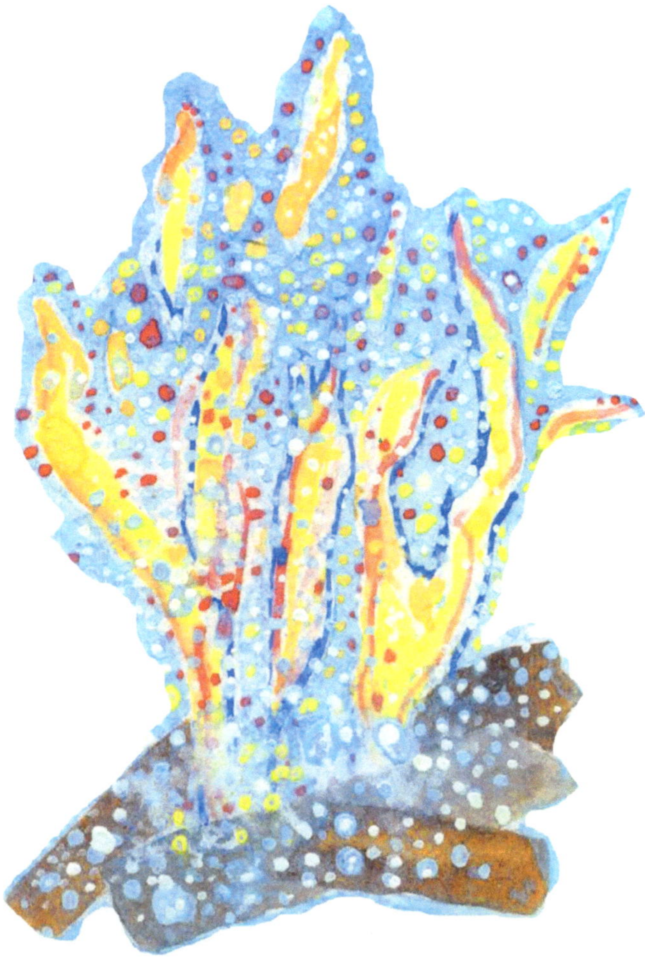

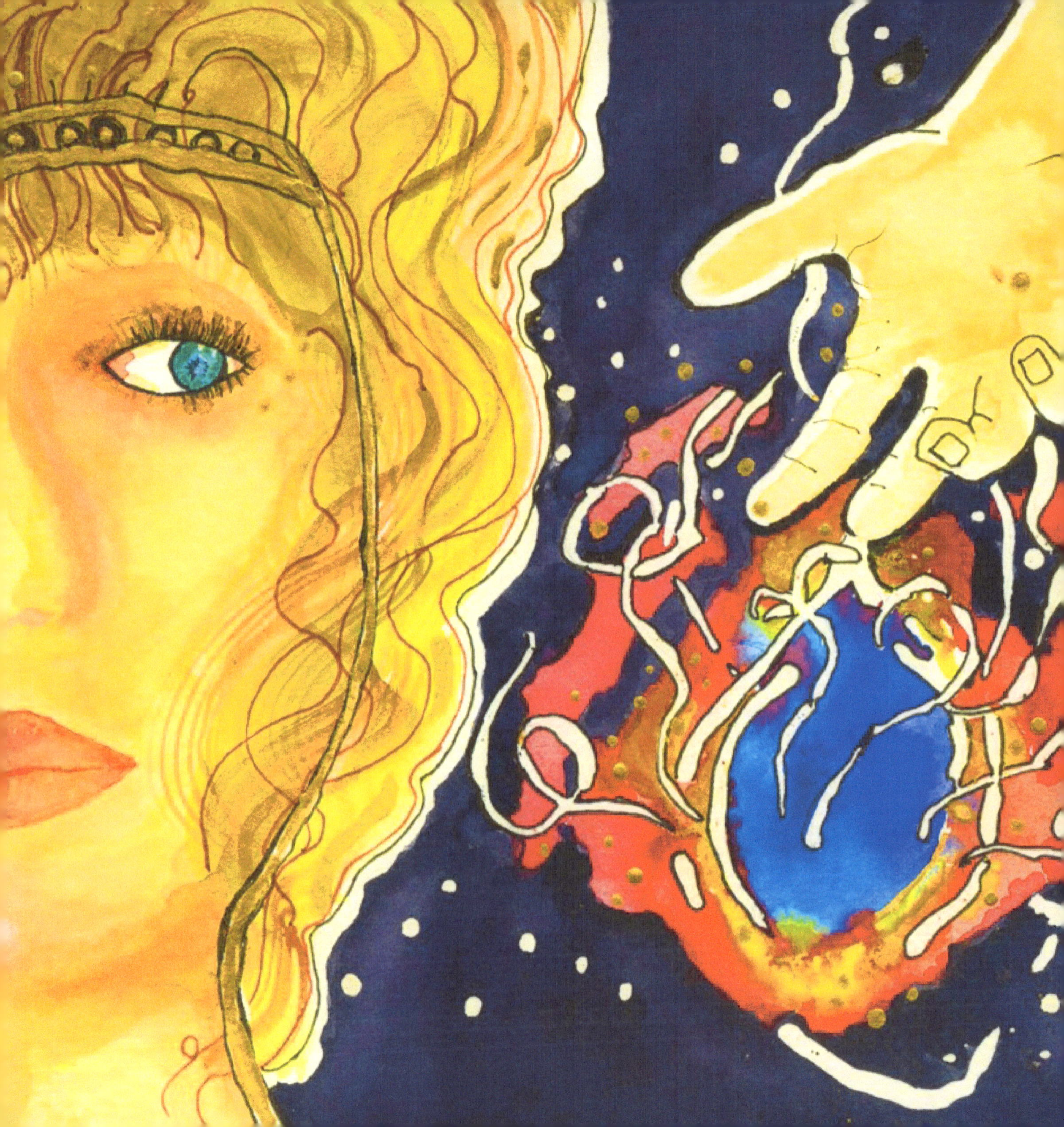

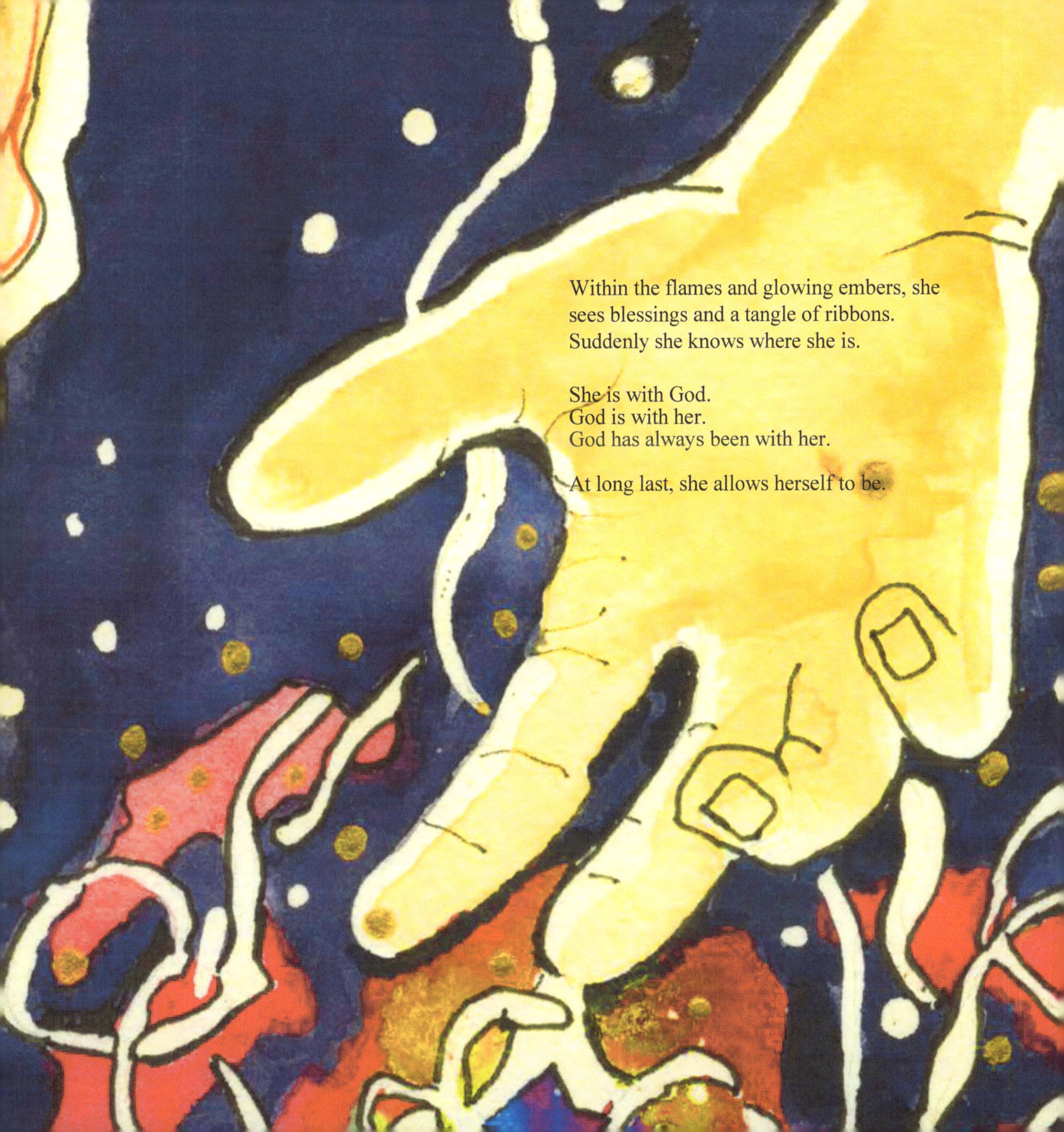

Within the flames and glowing embers, she sees blessings and a tangle of ribbons. Suddenly she knows where she is.

She is with God.
God is with her.
God has always been with her.

At long last, she allows herself to be.

Tonia Colleen Martin

This story took longer to live than to transcribe. For daydreamers, truth-seekers, joy-feeders, and those longing to let your heart instruct your mind, this little book is for you. Falling into my own stylized category of children's book for adults, *Intents and Purposes,* chronicles the path of a life abandoned by disconnection and loneliness as it moves to the threshold of hope and contentment.

Both text and illustrations are mine. Although countless versions reside in my constantly reconfiguring memory, this compilation seems to be its truest version.

I earned my MFA in Writing from Vermont College of Fine Arts, received the Hallberg Award for Art; Best of Show, Blue Line Gallery, Membership Medley; published in The Arts in Religious and Theological Studies; Ruminate Magazine; Metonym; Sierra College Journal.

tonia.colleen@gmail.com
FB: Mining With a Feather
www.toniacolleenmartin.com

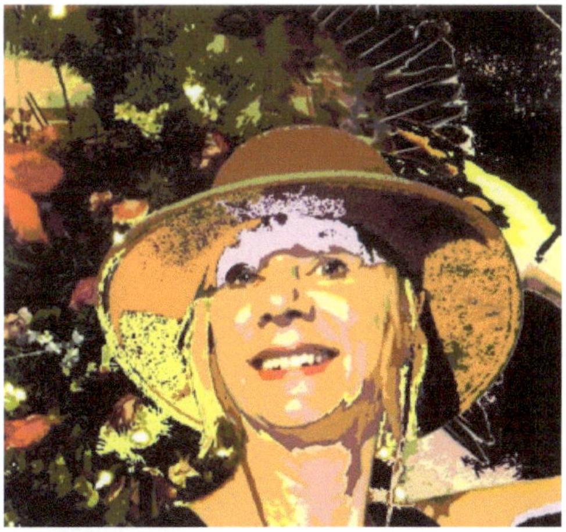

www.ingramcontent.com/pod-product-compliance
Ingram Content Group UK Ltd.
Pitfield, Milton Keynes, MK11 3LW, UK
UKHW061031310726
14089UKWH00009B/185
* 9 7 8 1 0 8 7 8 5 3 4 5 1 *